Ethics of Food

Processing Your Food

John Bliss

Heinemann Library
Chicago, Illinois

www.heinemannraintree.com
Visit our website to find out
more information about
Heinemann-Raintree books.

To order:
☎ Phone 888-454-2279
🖥 Visit www.heinemannraintree.com
to browse our catalog and order online.

Edited by Adam Miller, Andrew Farrow, and Adrian
Vigliano
Designed by Ryan Frieson
Illustrated by Mapping Specialists, Ltd. and
Planman Technologies
Picture research by Tracy Cummins
Originated by Capstone Global Library Ltd.
Printed and bound in the United States of America
by Corporate Graphics in North Mankato,
Minnesota
15 14 13 12 11
10 9 8 7 6 5 4 3 2 1

**Library of Congress Cataloging-in-Publication
Data**
Cataloging-in-Publication data is on file at the
Library of Congress.

ISBN 978-1-4329-5103-0 (HB)
ISBN 978-1-4329-6193-0 (PB)

Acknowledgements

The author and publisher are grateful to the
following for permission to reproduce copyright
material: AP Photo p. 13 (Mark Humphrey); Corbis
pp. 11 (© Corbis), 21 (© Dominique Derda), 35
(© Bettmann), 42 (© TWPhoto); Food Standards
Agency p. 50 top (food.gov.uk); Getty Images pp.
6 (DEA/G. LOVERA), 9 (Miguel Villagran), 20
(Graeme Robertson), 25 (Brandi Simons), 26 (Hans
Neleman); istockphoto p. 18 (© ALEAIMAGE);
Library of Congress Prints and Photographs
Division p. 38; mypyramid.gov p. 50 top; Rex
Features p. 28 (C. Magnolia/Everett); Shutterstock
pp. 5 (© Morgan Lane Photography), 17 (© Dmitriy
Kuzmichev), 23 (© Picsfive), 27 (© Helga Esteb), 30
(© Alen), 32 (© 29september), 36 (© Picsfive), 41
(© Kheng Guan Toh), 44 (© Dmitry Kalinovsky), 46
(© Noam Wind).

Cover photograph of a pig being processed
reproduced with permission of Getty Images (Scott
Olson).

We would like to thank Christopher Nicolson for
his invaluable help in the preparation of this book.

Every effort has been made to contact copyright
holders of any material reproduced in this book.
Any omissions will be rectified in subsequent
printings if notice is given to the publisher.

Contents

Some words are printed in bold, **like this**. You can find out what they mean by looking in the glossary.

What Is Processed Food?

The ethics of processed foods

Today, there are more people to feed around the world than ever before. In **developed countries**, even people living in small towns have access to thousands of different food products.

Most people like having a choice about the foods they eat, and processing foods into different products provides that. Processing has also made many foods more affordable for a wider range of people. Poor people often can more readily buy a can of vegetables than the same amount of fresh produce from a local farm. But critics say processed foods can present health problems, because they are loaded with ingredients known to cause disease. Fat, salt, and sugar are at the top of the "danger" list. Processed foods can be both a benefit and a risk.

Almost everything we eat requires some sort of processing. For example, you cannot eat a grain of wheat. Rather, the wheat needs to be **milled** into flour, and the flour then needs to be combined with other ingredients and baked in an oven before it becomes bread.

So, what is processing? Processing occurs in many ways for different reasons. Canning or freezing fruits or vegetables helps preserve them. They last longer on a store's shelf than they could if they were left as they were when they were harvested. Drying certain foods, such as meats and fruit, serves the same purpose. And meals packaged in cans or cartons give shoppers an easy way to eat a variety of foods without having to take the time to follow recipes. Some of these packaged foods can also be eaten far from the kitchen, making them useful for people who are on the go. Some processing can make foods safer to eat. Milk, for example, is pasteurized, a process that kills harmful organisms. Processed foods are common, and often cheap and convenient. Still, in recent years, some food experts have said that too many people worldwide eat too many processed foods.

Processing is not always a bad thing. Some fruits and vegetables are better tasting and even healthier if processed in some way. For example, freezing is often a good form of processing. If vegetables are frozen in the correct way, they retain their vitamins. This makes them healthier to eat than unprocessed vegetables that have been sitting in a store for several days. But, as we will see, many other foods are processed to the point of not only losing all their nutritional value, but also of becoming unsafe to eat.

Fresh vegetables are a great food choice, if they're available. In some places, vegetables that have been processed into cans are the only option for shoppers.

The history of processed food

People have been cooking food for over two million years. Cooking is a basic kind of food processing. Beyond that, the first kinds of food processing were probably used to make beer and bread. Both were invented about 10,000 years ago. Here, simple grains were processed into new foods or drinks that no longer resembled the original source. The role of yeast, which turns grain into beer, was likely an accidental discovery.

Over time, many methods of food processing were developed to preserve foods. Before refrigeration, people had to find ways to store foods that could spoil, such as meats, fruits, and vegetables. Meats were preserved through salting and air **curing** at least 2,500 years ago. (With air curing, the air itself dries the food to preserve it. Other forms of curing use chemicals to do the same thing.)

The ancient Romans enjoyed sausages and other cured meats. Salted fish, such as cod, were a mainstay of travelers in the 16th century, and native peoples in both South and North America made versions of jerky. Even fruitcake was invented as a way of preserving fruits and nuts. In the early 19th century, canning was invented as a way to process food so that it could be preserved.

Ancient Egyptians were familiar with the process of using grain and fruit to make beer and wine.

Modern processing techniques

Today, some of these traditional methods of preservation are still used. But many have been replaced by using chemicals and other food **additives**. One of the oldest **preservatives**, salt, is still used today. It's sometimes listed on food labels as some form of **sodium**. The human body needs some salt to function properly. But the large amounts found in some processed foods can increase the risk of high-blood pressure, which can lead to heart-related diseases.

Other common preservatives are nitrates and nitrites. Nitrates appear naturally in many vegetables. When added to food, especially meats, they help keep them from spoiling. But some experts say too many nitrates and nitrites could raise the risk of cancer. Others say these are safe at the levels used in food processing.

Two related chemicals called BHT and BHA are found in many foods. They help stop the fats found in foods from going bad. Processed foods are often high in fat, because food companies know humans are drawn to it. It adds flavor to food. And like salt, some fat is necessary for a healthy body. But the level of fat in processed foods is too high, a British government health institute said in 2010. The BHA and BHT added to foods may also pose health risks. Large doses have led to cancer in rats.

Other substances added to food include different fats. But one kind, called **trans fats**, is particularly unhealthy. Trans fats are found in oils called **partially hydrogenated oils**. These oils help preserve the food so it can sit longer on a shelf, and they appear in such products as margarine, baked goods, and snack foods. But trans fats have been linked to heart disease.

Many processed foods also lack something helpful to humans—**fiber**. Fruits, vegetables, and grains contain fiber, which helps the body to digest food and may reduce the risk of certain cancers. Processing these foods removes or reduces the fiber in them.

Some additives are natural and pose no health risks. Citric acid, for example, comes from citrus fruits. It's added to certain foods to keep their level of acid stable. Folic acid, a type of B vitamin, is added to certain foods because it has health benefits. The vitamin helps prevent heart disease. But some doctors and food experts worry about the additives and preservatives that may damage a person's health. They argue that people should eat fewer processed foods so they can avoid these harmful ingredients. Eating more fresh food from local sources is one way to do this. But food companies and others argue that not all people have access to that kind of food—or can afford it.

Processing Grains

Flour is a staple of human existence. All western cultures enjoy some kind of bread, and for many years, bread was at the center of people's diets. But the flour used by Europeans 1,000 years ago is very different from the flour at your local supermarket today.

The basic process of milling wheat into flour is fairly simple. The grains are ground between heavy rollers, which separate the **bran**, or outer coating, from the inner wheat **kernel** and **germ**. The germ is the center portion of the kernel, which contains the "embryo" of a new wheat plant. It also contains many important nutrients, including **protein**, vitamins, and healthy **fatty acids**. (Found in the fat of many animals and plants, fatty acids have many health benefits. Omega-3, for example, helps the brain function well.) In the past, when wheat was ground between stone wheels, the germ was crushed and became part of the rest of the milled kernel.

But today, many people buy and eat something called white flour. In white flour, the germ has been removed. But why remove the germ? The germ contains oils, which can go bad. By removing the germ, the shelf life of the flour is increased, meaning it can last much longer on a store shelf. The process of creating white flour also removes any illness-causing mold and fungus that might be on the grains. But unfortunately, removing the germ also removes much of the nutrition.

Health watch

Bye-bye bread

In 1972, Dr. Robert Atkins introduced a new diet designed to help people lose weight quickly. He stressed eating more meat and cutting down on bread, pasta, and even some vegetables. The Atkins Diet exploded in popularity during the 1990s, and many people on the diet completely stopped eating bread. Most dieters did lose weight, but many later put the pounds back on. And several doctors questioned the Atkins diet's long-term health effects. Dr. Robert H. Eckel of the University of Colorado said he and others "worry that the diet promotes heart disease...There is also potential loss of bone, and the potential for people with liver and kidney problems to have trouble with the high amounts of protein in these diets." The Atkins diet, however, still has many followers.

These pipes are part of a flour mill in Munich, Germany.

Enriching

In the 1920s, scientists began to realize that, while processed flour did not make people sick, it also was not particularly nutritious. So, companies started to **enrich** flour, meaning to put back the minerals and vitamins lost during processing. Enriching became popular, and in the 1940s the U.S. Army announced that it would only buy enriched flour. It began to make financial sense for processors to enrich their flour.

Golden rice

For much of the world, especially Asia, rice is the primary grain that people eat. Like white flour, white rice is created by removing the nutrient-rich husk, bran, and germ from brown rice. This is done to prevent spoiling—but, unfortunately, it also removes many of the health benefits of brown rice.

Since the late 1990s, scientists have been working on a new form of rice known as "golden rice." Golden rice contains beta-carotene, a mineral that converts to vitamin A inside the body. Scientists are creating golden rice to try to help countries where a lack of vitamin A is a problem.

Fortified food

If you look at a typical box of breakfast cereal, you will probably notice a claim such as "**fortified** with 18 vitamins and minerals." When food is fortified, processing adds nutrients that were never originally in the food. Many of the foods people buy in the grocery store have been fortified. Milk is usually fortified with vitamin D, orange juice is often fortified with calcium and vitamin D, and many cereals and grain products have been fortified with other vitamins and minerals.

Why has this food been fortified? For most of history, people did not have year-round access to necessary vitamins. This was largely because fruits and vegetables do not naturally grow in all areas at all times. People often suffered from diseases like rickets, caused by a lack of vitamin D, or scurvy, caused by a lack of vitamin C.

Fortifying foods allows people to have access to necessary nutrients, even in areas where little food is grown. However, doctors and scientists are starting to wonder how useful fortification is. There is some evidence that the body does not absorb nutrients from fortified foods the same way that it does when those minerals are found in foods naturally. Some fortified foods also have so much sugar and artificial flavoring added that they cease being healthy overall.

However, many people object to the development of golden rice, and to plans to grow it in **developing countries**.

Some people argue that it would be better to simply help citizens of developing countries gain access to naturally occurring vitamin-rich foods in their area. They also worry that introducing a **genetically modified (GM)** crop like golden rice presents the same range of issues that are connected to other GM crops. These concerns include possible health problems caused by eating these crops. (For more on GM crops and related concerns, see pages 20 and 21.)

Vitamins and minerals are often added to children's cereals, but so are unnecessary colors, sugars, and flavors.

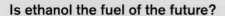

Environment watch

Is ethanol the fuel of the future?

The first Model T car designed by Henry Ford, in 1908, ran on ethanol, otherwise known as grain alcohol. Ethanol can be made from corn, wheat, grass, sugarcane, and even sawdust.

Today, ethanol is often proposed as an alternative fuel source to petroleum-based fuels like gasoline. While ethanol can be made in small batches fairly easily, a lot of energy is used to produce enough ethanol to serve as a substitute for gasoline. Critics argue that it actually takes more energy to produce the ethanol than it does to use gas in cars.

King corn

Corn on the cob, creamed corn, corn bread—corn has always been an important and delicious part of many people's diets in the West. Corn was first grown in the Americas, and it later spread to Europe and northern Africa. By 1600, it had made its way to China and beyond.

Corn has always been useful. It can be eaten as a vegetable without any processing (although cooking helps), but it can also be stored and turned into a grain. It can go through a process known as **fermentation** and be turned into alcohol, including ethanol (see box at right). Corn husks can be turned into fuel, or they can be used for rugs and twine. The plant's leaves make good animal feed, and in the days of outhouses, corncobs were even used as toilet paper!

Today, believe it or not, corn is in a huge number of the products you will find in a modern grocery store—and in many products in other stores as well. Corn has become the most important grain today. But why?

Creating a new plant

You are probably familiar with the idea of dog breeds like Labradors and poodles. These are breeds that were created by mating dogs to create the most desirable traits in future dogs. More recently, existing breeds have been crossbred to create new, "hybrid" breeds like Labradoodles (Labrador plus poodle).

The same thing happens with plants. Plants can be bred in ways that create new kinds of plants or better or more useful varieties of the same plant. In some instances, creating new plants is not very profitable for large agriculture companies or seed companies. After all, once they sell people the new plant, people can use the seeds from that plant to grow their own in the future.

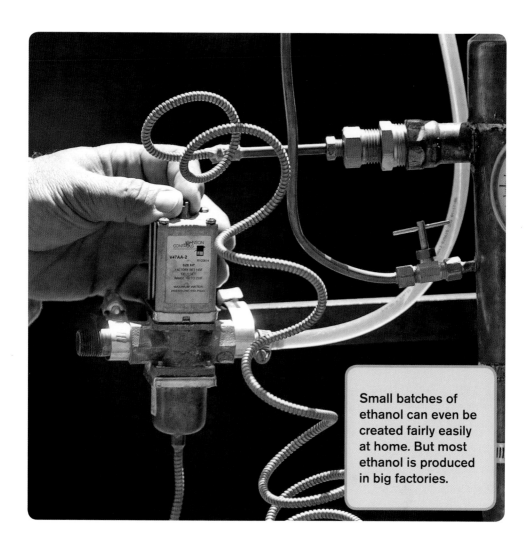

Small batches of ethanol can even be created fairly easily at home. But most ethanol is produced in big factories.

But, with corn, big agriculture companies discovered something important. New breeds of corn can be created in such a way that the new plants' seeds do not grow the same size of corn. So, a big company can crossbreed two varieties of corn to create a very desirable form of corn. Let's say they sell that corn to smaller farmers, who like the corn because it has big kernels. But that corn does not reproduce in the same way as other plants. This means the farmer has to buy more of the same corn from the big business every year.

Clearly, large agriculture companies can make a lot of money by creating new forms of corn. This makes them want to find new kinds of corn. Once they create the corn, they need to create more products to use those new types of corn.

Animal feed

Because it is so cheap and plentiful, people find new uses for corn. For example, it is processed into many animal feeds. Cattle, pigs, chicken, and even fish are all fed corn—even though cows and fish do not naturally eat corn (see pages 24 and 25). Those animals then become food for people, increasing the amount of corn we eat in our processed foods.

High fructose corn syrup (HFCS)

The use of corn that has lately been in the news most frequently is **high fructose corn syrup (HFCS)**. It was first developed in 1957, but HFCS was not really used before the 1970s. Today, 500 million bushels of corn are turned into 8.2 billion kilograms (18 billion pounds) of HFCS every year.

From the point of view of food producers, HFCS is a wonderful sugar substitute. It is inexpensive, easy to produce, and aids in keeping food moist. But there are serious downsides.

HFCS and obesity

There is a lot of conflicting information about the link between HFCS and **obesity**, or being severely overweight. It is clear that obesity rates have increased since HFCS became popular, but definitions of "obese" have also changed during this time period.

Health watch

Making HFCS

How is HFCS made? Food producers use the following steps:

1. Corn kernels are soaked in warm water containing the chemical sulfur dioxide. This makes the kernels softer and easier to separate.

2. The germ of the corn, which contains oil and nutrients, is removed (much like it is in white flour; see page 8).

3. The remaining cornstarch is washed.

4. Substances called enzymes are added to break the starch into substances called glucose and **fructose**.

5. The resulting syrup goes through an evaporation process so that it becomes ideal for shipping.

Because so much of the information comes from companies with an interest in selling either HFCS or competing products, it can be very difficult to know what is and isn't true.

However, there are some things we know:

- Because HFCS is cheaper than sugar, products with HFCS tend to come in larger serving sizes.

- Fructose does not stimulate leptin, a **hormone** that lets people know when they are full. So, people may overeat foods with HFCS.

- HFCS is found in many products where people may not expect it to be. So, some people who believe they are eating healthily actually are not.

Products that often contain forms of corn		
Food	Personal care	Industrial
Chewing gum	Medicines	Engine fuel
Candy	Deodorant	Plastics
Icing	Makeup	Chemicals
Instant tea	Vitamins	Explosives
Nondairy creamer		Shoe polish
Peanut butter		Glue
Alcohol		Fiberglass

Corn is found in food products—as well as in many unexpected places. This chart shows a few of the many items that contain corn.

Health watch

Battling over HFCS

No one disputes that using HFCS makes certain foods cheaper. But its use in so many foods—and its possible role in increasing certain diseases—has raised concerns. In the United States some people have called for banning the sale of products that contain the sugar. Some lawmakers in New York proposed such a ban in 2010. Rather than risk losing sales, some companies are beginning to take high-fructose corn syrup out of their foods and use other sugars instead. To some scientists, the larger issue is that too many people eat too much sugar in all forms.

Processing Fruits and Vegetables

Few things are healthier than fresh fruits and vegetables. But what happens when fruits and vegetables are processed?

From vine to can

Let's begin by looking at the example of tomatoes. Processed tomatoes—including canned tomatoes, ketchup, tomato paste, and tomato sauce—are a huge U.S. business. In 2001, $228 million worth of processed tomatoes were exported to other countries (Canada being the biggest customer). In 2007, the total value of U.S. processed tomatoes was $901 million. California is the biggest producer of processed tomatoes.

Processed tomatoes usually have a thicker skin than fresh-market tomatoes (those that are meant to be bought raw in the store). This is to help the tomatoes survive the mechanical harvesting and bulk transportation they undergo.

Health watch

Are canned fruits and vegetables safe?

Many people wonder whether or not canned fruits and vegetables are safe. In the case of tomatoes, the good news is that processed tomatoes appear to retain much of their health benefits. **Organic** products (those that are grown naturally, without chemicals) have the most lycopene and vitamins, but even non-organic tomato products have health benefits.

The bad news is that a chemical known as Bisphenol A (BPA) has been found in the linings of some canned foods. Among the concerns about BPA is that it can cause birth defects, obesity, and **neurological** issues. Many people worry that the acid in tomatoes may cause that chemical to leak into canned tomatoes.

In 2010 Canada became the first country to declare BPA a toxic substance. Also in 2010, the food company General Mills announced that it had found an alternative lining free of BPA. Companies around the world have already begun to remove or reduce the amount of BPA in food related products.

In modern farming, tomatoes, like most food plants, are grown and harvested in many different ways depending on their intended usage.

After transportation there is a very small period of time (about six hours) to turn the fresh tomatoes into paste without spoilage or damage. Because of this small window of time, the manufacturing plant (factory) is usually close to where the tomatoes are grown. Once the tomatoes have been turned into paste, it can be stored for up to 18 months. The manufacturer then sells the tomato paste to other companies that add spices, flavors, and colors to turn the industrial tomato paste into products like ketchup or tomato sauce.

The demand for processed tomatoes is expected to continue to grow. This is partly because condiments like salsa and ketchup are becoming more and more popular. It is also because tomatoes are rich in vitamins A and C, as well as the **antioxidant** lycopene, which some research suggests helps prevent cancer.

Ethylene

Ethylene is the naturally occurring gas that causes fruits (like tomatoes and bananas) and vegetables to ripen and decay. But food companies have found a way to process fruits and vegetables using ethylene.

Fruits and vegetables that will be transported and sold are often picked before they are ripe. These fruits and vegetables are then exposed to human-made ethylene to aid in their ripening process. So, even some fresh fruits now undergo a form of processing before getting to your plate.

How are baby carrots "born"?

Ethylene is not the only way that fruits and vegetables have become processed. For example, "baby carrots" are not actually baby carrots. They are regular carrots that have been peeled, cut into short lengths, and run through a grinder. They were first introduced in the 1980s by a California farmer who was tired of discarding imperfect carrots that could not be sold in grocery stores.

Baby carrots are generally as healthy as regular carrots. Some nutrients are lost in the peeling of the carrot, but given that most people peel carrots before eating them anyway, this does not have an enormous impact on the health benefits. However, baby carrots are much more expensive than regular carrots.

Baby carrots are delicious and nutritious, but they also undergo unnecessary processing.

Health watch

Added colors

Fruit juices and canned fruits and vegetables often have color added. In July 2010, the European Union began requiring that the following warning be placed on six food color additives: "Warning: Alurra Red AC E129 [or one of the other five colors] may have an adverse effect on activity and attention in children." In addition to Alurra Red (also called Red 40) the others are Ponceau 4R, Tartrazine (Yellow 5), Sunset Yellow FCF/Orange Yellow S (Yellow 6), Quinoline Yellow, and Carmoisine.

The warning labels are the result of a 2007 research study at the University of Southampton, in England. There were two parts to the study. In one, 153 three-year-olds and 144 eight- and nine-year-olds were given one of two drink mixes containing either **synthetic** (artificial) food colors and additives or a placebo, meaning a version with nothing added. The children were drawn from the general population and across a range of hyperactivity and attention deficit/hyperactivity disorder (ADHD) levels.

Researchers eventually concluded that the artificial food colors and additives increased hyperactive behavior in the children, at least up to middle childhood.

A more natural source

To avoid ethylene and other preservatives, some consumers choose to buy fresh, locally grown fruits and vegetables. Farmers' markets have become a popular source for those foods, as well as meat, dairy products, and other goods. Farmers within a community come to a public area, often a park, to sell their most recently harvested goods. The markets give shoppers the chance to support local people, rather than large companies that might be based thousands of miles away. At both these markets and in stores, some people look for organic foods. These foods are grown without any chemicals to kill insects or weeds or improve the soil. Organic meat and other animal products come from livestock fed food that does not contain chemicals. Organic foods and other food from local farms tend to be more expensive, as more work has to be done by hand. But people who can afford local or organic foods like knowing where their food comes from, and also that it does not have chemicals or preservatives in it.

GMs and Frankenfruits

Every living thing, including plants and animals, is made up of genes. These genes are passed from generation to generation and act as a code for different traits. Some of these traits are physical things, like eye color or hair color.

Fruits and vegetables are also made up of genes, and scientists have found ways to alter these genes to create more desirable features. For example, a farmer might want plants that are resistant to herbicides (poisons that kill plants), or that last through cold weather, or that resist bug infestation.

Organizations have developed to fight the spread of GM foods.

People have always altered plants through breeding. But today, scientists can actually add new genes to change a plant's genetic makeup. This process of creating new fruits and vegetables by mixing in genes from other fruits and vegetables is called genetic modification (GM). It has led to the name "Frankenfruit," which refers to the monster created by a doctor in Mary Shelley's novel *Frankenstein*.

The first GM crops to be grown were tomatoes. These tomatoes had been modified so that they would not become soft as easily. Soybeans, cotton, and corn have all also been modified for different reasons, such as heartier growth and more nutrition.

While GM foods may seem like a solution, many environmentalists and nutritionists are concerned about their side effects. For example, poisons are bred into some plants to help them resist pests. These poisons may actually be poisoning bugs and butterflies.

Health watch

Helpful human-made foods

Malnutrition, meaning the lack of enough nutrients, is a huge problem in poor African nations. The problem is especially bad among young children, since malnourished mothers cannot produce enough breast milk to feed their children. Powdered milk and formula are not good substitutes, as these require water and many villages do not have clean water supplies.

A French-designed processed food called Plumpy'nut was specifically designed to help feed malnourished children in Africa. It is a combination of peanut butter, powdered milk, and powdered sugar, enriched with vitamins and minerals. Because it is sweet, kids want to eat it. And because it does not need to be refrigerated or cooked, it is easy to store and serve. With this food, some malnourished children have been able to achieve a normal weight in only four weeks.

Plumpy'nut has become a lifesaving product for malnourished children all over the world.

Although people do not want bugs eating crops, they are still an important part of the natural order. Recent tests have shown that the crops not only poison pests that attempt to eat them, but they also leak the toxins from their roots into the ground.

Nutritionists are concerned about GM foods for two reasons. The first is that, although modifying crops may allow new nutrients to be added to foods, it may also introduce harmful chemicals.

The other concern has to do with allergies. In 1992 a U.S. company added genes from Brazil nuts to soybeans, in an attempt to create more nutritious soybeans. However, people who were allergic to Brazil nuts discovered that they were also allergic to the modified soybeans.

Approximately 70 percent of processed foods contain GM ingredients. Unless an ingredient panel lists not only every ingredient, but also how each ingredient has been modified, it could be impossible for a person with allergies to ever know if the food they are eating is safe for them.

Processing Meat

Meat has long been an important part of many people's diets. Early humans were hunters and gatherers. The connection they had to their meat was immediate and undeniable—they killed an animal and ate it. Later, they added the process of cooking.

When people began settling in communities and developed farming, their connection to their meat was still strong. Many people only ate meat they themselves hunted, while others ate meat that a friend or neighbor had hunted. Meat could be salted, cured, and stored (all forms of processing). Meat could be traded for grains, vegetables, or other needed products. But everyone knew where the meat on the table had come from.

In the 18th and 19th centuries, during a period known as the Industrial Revolution, major changes to agriculture and industry changed how people lived and worked. More and more people moved into cities. Although at first even city dwellers might have a couple of chickens in their yard, or even a cow for milk, people began getting more and more removed from their meat. People might go to the local butcher shop to buy their meat, but over time, most of these shops were not even owned by a local butcher.

GUSTAVUS SWIFT

Gustavus Swift (1839–1903) started his meat business with a simple meat market in Massachusetts. He quickly became a cattle buyer, and then a cattle wholesaler (selling cattle to other butchers). Swift is credited with the development of the first usable ice-cooled railroad car. This car allowed Swift's meatpacking company to ship meat throughout the country, ushering in the era of cheap beef.

Because he owned the cattle, the processing plant, the means of transportation, and the market, Swift controlled every aspect of his meat industry. This kind of business plan is known as vertical integration. Today, Swift & Company is the third-largest processor of fresh beef and pork products in the United States and is also the leading beef processor in Australia.

The majority of meats that are sold in an average grocery store have been processed in a huge, industrial facility like this one.

Today, most meat eaters are even further removed from their food. Most people buy meat in large grocery stores, where it has been frozen or pre-packaged into other foods. As we will see, industry and processing have entered every element of the meat we eat, from the way the animals are conceived, to what they are fed, to how they wind up on our plates.

The United States is the world's meatpacking center, with about 10 billion animals slaughtered there every year. In the European Union, the annual figure is 300 million cattle, sheep, and pigs and 4 billion chickens. Today, just a few processors—Tyson, Swift, Cargill, and National Beef—control 80 percent of the market. This gives them the power to control how meat is both raised and processed.

What cows eat

Like all mammals, a baby cow drinks its mother's milk. After being weaned from milk, though, cows are naturally plant eaters. Left to nature, cows will graze in pastures. Cows, sheep, and other animals called ruminants have the ability to turn simple grass, which humans cannot digest, into protein. A cow's rumen (its second stomach) is host to a variety of bacteria that can break the grass down into protein. A cow's manure (waste) provides excellent fertilizer for the grass, so the grass continues to grow—and the whole process continues.

As natural as eating and fertilizing grass is, it is not the most cost-effective process for creating meat. This is because grass alone does not allow cows to grow as quickly as other diets. Two generations ago, cows were not slaughtered until they were four or five years old. One generation ago, they were slaughtered at two or three years old. Today, most cows born to become meat have only a 16-month lifespan. This is accomplished by feeding the cow a diet made primarily of corn and growth hormones. Because cows do not naturally digest corn, they also need to be given regular doses of antibiotics to aid the digestion process.

When we eat cows that are raised this way, or drink their milk, these antibiotics eventually make their way into our own bodies. Over time, bacteria evolve to resist the antibiotics, so the drugs are no longer effective. Many doctors worry that these new, stronger bacteria could make humans sick. The antibiotics people use to fight illness are often the same ones given to the cows. If the evolved bacteria entered a human, doctors would not have antibiotics strong enough to kill them. Or the drugs that can kill the bacteria are much more expensive than regular antibiotics.

Doctors also have expressed concerns that the growth hormones fed to cows are making their way to our bodies, causing issues like increased obesity and early-onset puberty.

The issue of eating animals that were raised with the help of growth hormones has been dealt with in different ways around the world. For example, in the United States various forms of naturally-occurring and artificial growth hormones are approved for use in the raising of livestock. But other countries have taken an opposite approach. For instance, the feeding of growth hormones to cattle has been banned in the European Union since 1988. In the UK, the ban was in place in December 1986. The ban also applies to any meat imported into the UK from countries such as the United States.

Health watch

Is corn-fed beef unhealthy?

Even without the antibiotics and hormones, would corn-fed beef still be unhealthy to eat? A growing body of evidence suggests that it would be. The beef from corn-fed cattle has fewer omega-3 fatty acids than grass-fed beef. Omega-3 fatty acids are necessary for human development. They help in brain development and may reduce the risk of heart disease. The human body is not able to make these fatty acids, so they have to be provided by foods.

Another problem with corn-fed beef is that it has more fat than grass-fed beef. Also, because corn-fed cattle often live in small, enclosed pens, they live in their own manure. If their manure contains **E. coli** or other harmful bacteria, it can wind up back on the cow—and thus in the cow's meat. (See page 28 for a tragic example of this danger.)

Although cows cannot naturally digest corn, it has become a major part of their feed.

The kill floor

Killing an animal for food will never be pleasant. But modern slaughter practices for animals are so **industrialized** that they have become cruel to animals, unsafe to people who do the work, and unsafe to people who eat the meat.

In an industrial "kill floor," cattle pass onto the floor in a chute that forces them to walk in a single-file line. The walls of the chute are high enough that the animal cannot see much more than the rear end of the cow in front of it. Eventually, they move onto a conveyor belt, much like a moving sidewalk in an airport. The cows actually straddle this conveyor, rather than standing on it.

In a modern slaughterhouse, the chute that leads to the kill floor is narrow enough that cattle cannot see what lies ahead.

The stunner

Above the belt, on a raised platform, stands a person called a stunner. The stunner carries a pneumatic gun, which uses air power to propel a steel bolt into the head of the animal. Although this person is called a stunner, his or her job is to kill the cow, not just stun it. Unfortunately, the stun does not always kill the cow. There have been reports of cattle waking up farther down the process. A second stunner is available farther down the process to ensure that cattle are killed as painlessly as possible.

After the animal passes the stunner, a worker ties a cord around one of its back legs. The other end of the cord is attached to an overhead trolley, or moving track. The animal is carried upside-down to the bleeding area, where a worker cuts its throat. While reflexes cause the animal to kick and jerk, it is dead at this point.

TEMPLE GRANDIN

Dr. Temple Grandin (born 1947) is a professor of animal science who has designed livestock-handling facilities in North America, Europe, and Australia. Grandin's designs draw in part on her own experiences of living with autism. Autism is a disorder that affects the development of the brain. Some people with autism function very well, while others may have extreme difficulty with social interaction and communication. As a child, Grandin often felt overwhelmed by the multitude of sights and sounds surrounding her. She related her own feelings to those of the cattle on the ranch where she was raised. She realized that limiting the sensory experiences the animals were exposed to would help calm them.

Today, Grandin's designs for slaughterhouses are used to handle half the cattle in the United States. Companies such as Burger King and McDonald's have hired Grandin to observe and assess the slaughter of cattle they own at the National Beef Plant. According to Grandin, since McDonald's became interested in the welfare of its cattle, the process has become more humane.

Temple Grandin at an awards ceremony in 2010. In 2009, a critically acclaimed movie, *Temple Grandin*, was released. It told the story of her fascinating life.

Case study:
A terrible tragedy

In the summer of 2001, Barbara and Michael Kowalcyk went on vacation with their four children. Along the way, they stopped for hamburgers and other fast food.

Two weeks after they got home, their two-and-a-half-year-old son, Kevin, started suffering from diarrhea and a mild fever. When the Kowalcyks saw blood in Kevin's diarrhea, they rushed him to the emergency room. Doctors discovered Kevin had a form of E. coli, a type of food poisoning named for the bacteria that cause it. E. coli is sometimes found in ground meat and other processed foods. While it is dangerous for all people, it is especially deadly to young and elderly people. Twelve days after being admitted to the hospital, Kevin died.

On August 1, the day after Kevin went to the hospital, the meat packing plant that had processed the beef the Kowalcyks had eaten tested positive for E. coli **contamination**. Because of this experience, Barbara Kowalcyk became a food activist, fighting for rules and regulations to improve food safety in the United States.

Kevin's story points out some of the concerns about the safety of processed food. Many people fear that our food processing methods are not always safe. When a problem arises, it is often not detected until after one or more person gets sick. Even then, food **recalls** (removing food products from stores) come too late, or they are ineffective.

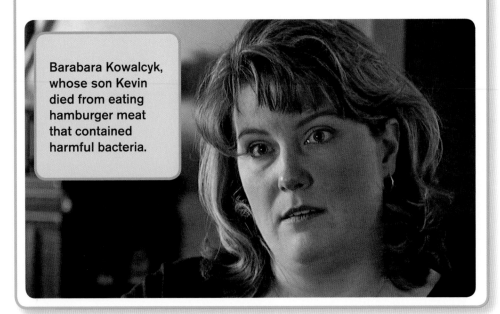

Barabara Kowalcyk, whose son Kevin died from eating hamburger meat that contained harmful bacteria.

Cannibal cows and mad cow disease

The meat products that come from large animals such as cows and hogs represent only part of the process. The rest of an animal's carcass is converted into a host of useful products. This process is called rendering. Until 1997 much of the product rendered from cattle, including meat and bone meal, was then fed back to the cattle. The theory was that protein was protein, so that even though cows do not naturally eat meat, there was no harm in feeding it to them.

In 1993 there was an outbreak of bovine spongiform encephalopathy (BSE). BSE is more commonly known as mad cow disease, because it makes cows act strange, or "mad." If a person eats a cow infected with BSE, he or she can develop a variation of a neurological disease (a disease affecting the brain, nerves, or spinal cord).

During the peak period of outbreak in the United Kingdom, almost 1,000 new cases of BSE were diagnosed every week. The first case of mad cow disease in the United States did not occur until 2003. It was discovered that one cause of BSE was that cows were eating the rendered product of other cows that were infected.

In 1997 the United States banned the practice of giving feed that had been made from other cows to cattle. In 2007 the U.S. government strengthened the rules about how animal feed must be made to further reduce instances of BSE. However, there are no rules preventing cow products from being made into animal feed for other animals, such as chickens or pigs. Some scientists worry that if a cow with BSE goes undiagnosed, it could infect other animals this way.

"Ground beef is not a completely safe product. Unfortunately it looks like we are going a bit in the opposite direction."—Dr. Jeffrey Bender, a food safety expert quoted in 2009, discussing problems with E. coli contamination

The industrialized chicken

The chicken industry is also a marvel of modern food processing. People have been breeding and crossbreeding chickens to develop desirable traits at least since the 1800s. In the late 1800s, the emerging railroad network made it easy to transport chickens from hatcheries to market. At the time, most of the chicken industry focused on eggs, rather than chicken as meat.

Health watch

What is a chicken nugget?

Chicken nuggets are a heavily processed food. Chicken nuggets were first invented in the 1950s. In 1979 McDonald's commissioned the food-processing company Tyson to create a recipe. The meat is held together with phosphate salts and then fried. Frozen chicken nuggets sold in grocery stores can be made either from white meat or from "mechanically separated chicken (MSC)." MSC is meat that has been mechanically taken off the bones or other parts of chicken. But really, chicken nuggets are more corn than meat. The meat comes from chickens that ate corn, a huge number of ingredients and additives in the nugget itself are corn-based, and even the dipping sauces served with the nuggets are made primarily from corn!

Experts have estimated that average chicken nuggets have around 37 ingredients, and that at least 30 of those ingredients come from corn.

Health watch

Food fight in the schools

Many children love chicken nuggets for a quick snack or school time meal. But to some food experts, they're just one of the many processed foods kids shouldn't be eating. Many school lunches contain highly processed foods with high levels of fat, sugar, and salt. And some schools have machines that sell similar foods, snacks, and drinks such as sodas all day long. In the United Kingdom, well-known TV chef Jamie Oliver led the battle to improve school lunches there and in other countries. Oliver called for more "naked" foods, meaning fresh fruits and vegetables, and fewer processed foods. He also said students should receive more food education, so they know which foods are the best for them to eat. In the United States, even the military has addressed the issue of school food. In 2010, a group of retired officers said the usual school lunches were making kids too fat—and making it harder for the military to find new recruits that met its weight guidelines. Studies by the government strongly suggested that eating school lunches made children fatter. Using fresh ingredients, however, drives up the cost of school meals. Some U.S. lawmakers opposed spending more money on new, healthier school-meal programs.

During the two world wars (1914–18 and 1939–45), the U.S. government encouraged people to raise chickens at home. A small flock of chickens could be an efficient way to discard table scraps, produce many eggs for protein, and supply meat. A chicken flock is very vulnerable to disease and parasites, so chicken remained much more expensive than other meat until the 1950s. At this point, antibiotics and other drugs began to be used to keep chickens healthy.

Drugs, combined with higher-protein and vitamin-enriched feed, helped create the era of large-scale chicken production that we have today. The chicken industry is estimated to have a total annual value of $40 billion. Today, hens are often housed in windowless buildings with 249,000 other chickens. Six or seven hens may share a cage so small that they cannot even spread their wings. Hens do not even sit on their own eggs, as incubation (keeping the eggs warm) is done by machine. Like other livestock, chickens are often fed growth hormones to increase their size.

Preservatives in meat

All meat is processed in some way, to get it off the animal and ready to sell. But the term "processed meat" usually refers to meat that is mixed with preservatives of some kind. Some of these meats include hot dogs, lunch meats such as bologna and ham, bacon, and a variety of canned meats.

For example, sausage is one of the oldest forms of processed meats. Sausages are typically made from pork. Traditional sausage is made by putting tissues and organ meat—which is highly fatty and nutritious, but a little gross to many people—into a casing made from the animal's own intestine. Today, the casing is frequently made from other materials such as collagen, cellulose, or even plastic.

Most processed meats have something in common: they have high levels of salt, fat, nitrates, and nitrites. These ingredients preserve the meat and keep it from spoiling, but also add health risks. A recent study suggests that all processed meats increase the risk of heart disease and diabetes, compared to unprocessed red meats such as beef, lamb, and pork. The study showed that the processed meats were four times as salty as the unprocessed meats and contained 50 percent more nitrates.

The expression "You don't want to see how the sausage is made" is often used to refer to something that you enjoy, but that has questionable roots.

The nitrates and nitrites in processed meats particularly concern many scientists. In large doses, they can be deadly to humans. Food companies must follow strict rules about how much they put in their meats. But even these so-called safe amounts could lead to health problems. In the body, nitrites combine with certain proteins to create **nitrosamines**. Some of these chemicals cause cancer in animals and could affect humans too. Consuming a lot of nitrates and nitrites has also been linked to other diseases in humans, such as Alzheimer's disease and some forms of diabetes. Some scientists, however, say the fear of getting a serious disease from eating nitrates and nitrites is overstated. And humans eat more nitrates in vegetables than they do in processed meats. Also, one study suggests eating nitrates and nitrites might actually strengthen heart cells.

Health watch

Fake fats

Because animals have fat, animal products are naturally fatty foods. As doctors began to make connections between eating too many fats and health problems such as heart disease, scientists began looking for alternatives to the fats that are naturally present in animal products.

Margarine, a kind of synthetic butter was created in 1869. Like many processed foods, it was created to help an army. Margarine was developed for the French army. Armies need to travel with their kitchens, and butter does not keep well without refrigeration. Synthetic or artificial fats are more stable than naturally occurring fats, so they do not require the kind of refrigeration that other fats do. Their structure can be controlled, giving these products a more consistent and reliable texture. They are also cheaper than natural fats.

In the 1990s Proctor & Gamble attempted to create a fat that would not add any calories to foods. The product was marketed as Olestra. Unfortunately, the reason Olestra does not add calories is that it is made of products that humans are not able to digest. Many people became ill after eating foods made with Olestra, but it can still be found in some processed food products.

Dangerous places to work

Slaughterhouses and the meatpacking industry have been areas of concern for centuries—but not just for the treatment of animals. Conditions for workers in meatpacking plants in the late 19th and early 20th centuries were horrible. Employees were overworked, and plants failed to maintain basic safety measures. Industrial accidents were common.

Conditions improved with the growth of **labor unions** in the 1930s and 1940s. But today, as the strength of the unions has diminished and the demand for processed meat has increased, the situation has worsened.

The human cost

Today, Human Rights Watch has called meatpacking and slaughterhouses the most dangerous factory jobs in the United States. Part of the problem is that meatpacking is treated as factory work. Workers perform a limited number of tasks, repeating them over and over again. They are often forced to work at a pace that is too fast to be safe. Working conditions are not **sanitary**, and workers often perform their jobs covered in animal blood, urine, and feces (waste).

Workers can suffer injuries from a slip of the knife, or from repeating the same motion more than 10,000 times a day. They occasionally pass out from the fumes of the chemicals used to process the meat. They have arms or legs crushed by unsafe machinery. They get infections from handling the meat, which results in their fingernails separating from their fingers. Temple Grandin (see page 27) has written that it is not uncommon for full-time slaughterhouse workers to become sadistic, meaning they take pleasure in being cruel. The process of constantly killing other living beings affects a person's behavior.

Because the people who work in these factories are poor (and sometimes in the United States illegally), they often do not have other options. Large packing plants tend to suppress workers' efforts to gain rights by forming unions, and they fire workers who support a union. Large meatpackers in the United States regularly advertise for workers in Mexico. If these workers come to the United States illegally, they risk being arrested and deported. The meatpackers and slaughterhouses that hire illegal workers rarely face significant punishments, even though it is illegal to knowingly hire someone who is in the country illegally.

Workers in the meat processing industry have long struggled to gain fair treatment and safe working conditions from their employers. These workers are holding a rally in Chicago in 1946.

Processing Dairy Products

Dairy products, another essential part of many people's diets, are the result of many processing steps.

For example, all cheese is processed food made from milk. Farmers used to make cheese at home, but today, cheese is created in a factory. The first step is to **pasteurize** the milk. Milk is heated to 74 °C (165 °F), killing harmful bacteria. (For more on pasteurization, see pages 38 and 39.) After the milk cools, it is pumped into a stainless steel vat, and a starter culture (or bacteria) is added to the milk. Large robotic arms stir the milk. Rennet, an animal byproduct, is added to the milk to thicken it.

The milk that goes into manufactured cheese may have come from hundreds of dairies.

After curds form, they are mechanically cut into thousands of small cubes. The curds and their whey (a clear liquid) are pumped into a trough-like tub called a finishing table. The curds are mounded into piles and begin to knit into a solid mass.

The whey is drained off and pumped into another machine, where it is condensed, meaning the liquids are removed. The whey is shipped to other processors, where it is used in products like candy, ice cream, and baked goods. (People with dairy allergies have to read ingredients very carefully, since dairy products like whey may turn up in processed foods that one would not expect to contain milk products.)

The cheese curds are mechanically cut and re-cut and combined with hot water. The cheese is melted into a big, shiny mound and then formed into mounds to cool. The mounds of cheese are soaked in a brine (salty water) bath, which is where different cheeses gain their different flavors. The cheese is then further processed and sold.

Cheese product

While clearly heavily processed and mechanized, the cheese described so far is not that different from cheese made in earlier times. However, what we think of as American cheese, or processed cheese, is a different product altogether.

The now-familiar orange slice of processed cheese was first created in Switzerland in 1911. James Kraft applied for a patent (exclusive right to make it) in 1916. Laughing Cow cheese, originally created in France, is another popular form of processed cheese.

Emulsifiers—substances that bind two different substances together—are added to the cheese product, which makes the cheese melt evenly. For this reason, these types of cheese are popular in cooking and for use with things like cheeseburgers. The U.S. Food and Drug Administration (FDA) recognizes three distinct forms of processed cheese:

• pasteurized process cheese

• pasteurized process cheese food

• pasteurized process cheese spread

The terms "pasteurized prepared cheese product" and "pasteurized process cheese snack" do not have U.S. Food and Drug Administration guidelines and can be used to describe almost any cheese-like product.

Case study:
Drunk cows and pasteurized milk

Until the mid-1800s, dairy cows lived on farms or on small patches of land in cities. If people drank milk, it most likely came from a cow that lived near them. As cities grew larger, lack of room and sanitation problems meant that fewer cows lived in cities. The first milk brought to New York City by train was in 1842.

Scientist Louis Pasteur made remarkable breakthroughs in discovering the causes of diseases, and in methods of disease prevention.

At that time, most milk was actually coming from cows that lived at alcohol breweries and distilleries. The cows lived there to eat the grain mash that was left over from making beer and alcohol. This feed had very little nutritional value, and as a result the milk from cows that ate it was of very poor quality. The public began to object to the idea of the horrible conditions the cows were kept in, and to the fact that children were drinking milk produced by "drunk cows."

In 1862 New York banned the sale of the "drunk" milk, and many other cities began to follow this example. The solution was to have cows live in grassy areas around the city and then transport the milk to the city. But because the source of the milk—farms—was now so far away from the customer, problems began to occur with milk. People created some of these problems—for example, they would add chalk to milk to make it appear whiter and even add poisonous formaldehyde to keep the milk from souring. Milk improperly transported also began to develop and create diseases.

During the late 1800s, researchers Robert Koch and Louis Pasteur developed the germ theory of disease. This theory states that tiny organisms such as bacteria, which the scientists called germs, cause many diseases. They discovered that disease could easily be spread by contaminated food. Milk, which arrived from the country daily and was consumed raw, was seen as a cause.

Pasteurizing milk (heating it to very high temperatures to kill the bacteria) was seen as a solution to the problem of diseases spread by milk. In 1909 Chicago became the first city to prohibit selling unpasteurized milk, and other cities followed suit. Later, **homogenization** also became a standard procedure. In this process, the cream (fat) globules in milk are broken up into tiny particles. This keeps a cream layer from forming at the top of milk.

It has been shown that pasteurizing milk not only destroys the germs, but also destroys some of the nutrients. Critics have also worried that because pasteurizing destroys evidence of germs, there is no way to tell if a farm is unsanitary. Still others lament that the very act of pasteurization has added a step, or process, into what used to be a simple food product. Making even the most simple of foods into a product requiring technology alienates us from our food, making it difficult for people to tell the difference between food as it exists naturally and processed food. This means people are increasingly cut off from the food they eat, and as a result may be less able to notice the difference between real and processed food. Because of that, some critics worry that people might lose sight of how unhealthy some processed foods can be.

Raw milk and cheese

With products like fluorescent orange "pasteurized prepared cheese product" available in cans in grocery stores, it is no wonder that many people are looking to raw milk and raw cheese as more natural alternatives.

Raw milk is the natural, unchanged milk that has not been pasteurized, homogenized, or otherwise heated above the body temperature of the cow. Likewise, raw cheese is cheese that has been made from raw milk. However, while raw milk has to be consumed quickly to prevent spoiling, cheese made from raw milk has to be aged for at least 60 days to allow the acids and salts to kill the bacteria.

Although most states allow the selling of raw cheese, only 10 U.S. states allow raw milk to be sold in retail outlets. In other states, people can only buy raw milk directly from a farmer.

Why drink raw milk?

It must be said that some of the interest in raw milk is simply a fad. What people do and do not want to eat goes in and out of fashion in much the same way that clothing does.

Health watch

The push for cheese

At times, some U.S. government agencies have warned against eating too much cheese, since it's high in a kind of fat linked to heart disease and other illnesses. But producing cheese and selling foods that contain it is a big business. So the United States Department of Agriculture (USDA) has a program to help companies sell more cheese. In 2010, it worked with the Domino's Pizza restaurant chain to add cheese to some pizzas, and then advertize the cheesier pies. Other companies have also received government help to sell more cheese products. The government has also used ads, sometimes with film stars or famous athletes, to convince Americans to drink more milk. The cheese program in particular upset some doctors. Dr. Walter C. Willett of Harvard University said, "The USDA should not be involved in these programs that are promoting foods that we are consuming too much of already."

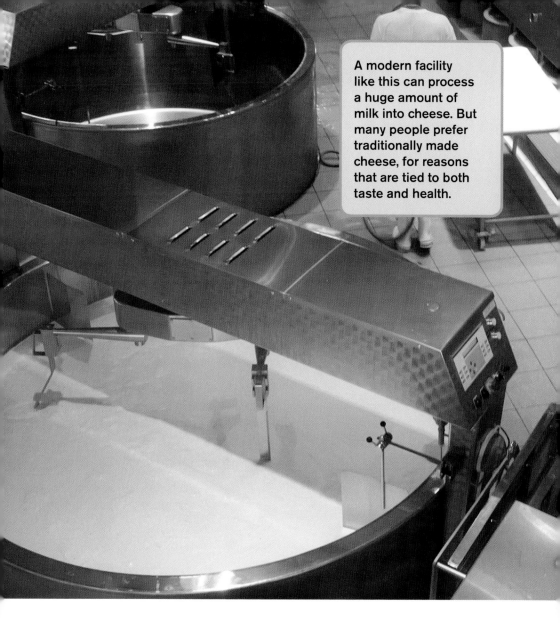

A modern facility like this can process a huge amount of milk into cheese. But many people prefer traditionally made cheese, for reasons that are tied to both taste and health.

But some people are genuinely interested in raw milk as a food that provides excellent nutritional value. Many people are seeking raw milk in an attempt to eat fewer processed foods. Others are concerned about the cows used to make most mass-produced milk. Most milk from dairy farms comes from Holstein cows. These cows have been bred to produce huge amounts of milk—more milk than their own calves need. The way they have been bred has also led to the need to give the cows antibiotics and growth hormones. Many people worry about the dangers posed when humans, especially young people who are still growing, ingest so many antibiotics and hormones with their milk.

What Does It All Cost?

Think about all the products you see at your local supermarket. How many of them are ready-to-eat, processed foods? Just add milk or water, or pop them in the microwave for three minutes, and these foods are ready to go. Better yet, there are shelves and shelves of snack foods people can eat right out of the bag. Some products offer a complete meal, vacuum-sealed and ready to go. Kids on the go or parents looking for a quick meal solution can just drive through their local fast food outlet.

The snack foods and quick meals for sale at convenience stores are a cheap source of calories, but they often contain hidden costs.

These foods are appealing to people with busy schedules, and to families with two working parents and kids who are going straight from school to activities. Best of all, this food is cheap. But the foods have a hidden cost, and we are paying the price with our health.

Case study:
Changing the Aboriginal diet

In 1982 nutrition scientist Kerin O'Dea undertook a research project in Western Australia. He recruited a group of 10 Aborigines—the native people of Australia—for his study. These people had all grown up in the Australian bush, and they now lived in and around the town of Derby. All were middle-aged and overweight, and they all suffered some of the health problems commonly associated with a diet of processed food. They were **diabetic**, had high blood pressure, and showed risk factors for heart disease. Their diet was common for the area: processed sugar, processed flour, processed rice, carbonated drinks, meat, and potatoes.

O'Dea accompanied the group back to their native homeland in North West Australia. There they returned to the eating methods they had grown up with, such as hunting and gathering all of their food. Instead of eating the heavily processed sugars and **carbohydrates** they had grown used to, their diet consisted of fish, birds, and local vegetables.

After seven weeks of this new lifestyle, O'Dea performed a series of tests on his subjects. Their health had improved in every way. All had lost weight. Their blood pressure had dropped. Their **cholesterol** levels had fallen into the normal range. For many of them, their diabetes had completely disappeared. In less than two months, they had regained normal health.

The results were striking. While the increased activity in their new lifestyle no doubt contributed to their improved health, for O'Dea the conclusion was clear. It demonstrated the number of health issues that can be directly linked to diet.

Is processed food cheaper?

One of the reasons processed food is so appealing is because of its cost and convenience. For example, a typical box of brand-name macaroni and cheese that is made on the stove costs $1.29, plus the cost of adding small amounts of milk and butter. It makes a meal in less than 30 minutes.

Environment watch

Packaging

Food packaging is an often-overlooked byproduct of industrial food. It can become damaging to the environment.

Products are often packed in at least two layers of packaging, such as a bag within a box. Individual boxes are packed into larger boxes for shipping, and these boxes are often wrapped in layers of cellophane before being shipped. In the grocery store, fresh items, such as meat, may be packed on a Styrofoam tray that is wrapped in plastic. Labeling adds additional paper and glue to the package.

Packaging can even compromise the safety of food. In June 2010, Kellogg's recalled 28 million boxes of children's breakfast cereals after a number of people suffered from nausea and vomiting. The culprit turned out to be the inner liner of the box, which was leaching methylnaphthalene, a petroleum product, into the cereal.

This warehouse holds packaged food, waiting to be shipped to grocery stores.

How does this compare to making macaroni and cheese from scratch? Buying the noodles, cheese, flour, and milk (to make the sauce) separately may seem like it costs more, and it certainly takes more time. But, when divided by serving, it actually does not cost more.

But if people only have two dollars to spend, they are better off buying a pre-packaged, processed box. Since they cannot buy the fresh ingredients for the same price, buying the processed foods at least lets them eat dinner. If people are homeless and do not have access to regular refrigeration or storage facilities, they are also better off buying processed food. If people have limited space for food or lack good transportation to a grocery store, they may also wish to buy smaller pre-packaged foods instead of fresh ingredients.

Health watch

Finding food in a desert

In wealthy neighborhoods, shoppers often have a wide range of stores where they can buy their food. The largest of them offer tens of thousands of goods, usually at reasonable prices. The story is different, however, in the poor neighborhoods of large cities and in some rural areas. These communities are food deserts, meaning residents lack easy access to affordable and nutritious food. In some places, governments offer tax breaks to large supermarkets to place stores in food deserts. But at times, the companies still don't want to come, believing they cannot make enough money in those locations. In many city neighborhoods, the closest place to buy groceries is at a tiny corner store. These stores often lack the room for refrigerator cases that hold fruits and vegetables, so shoppers can't buy these items fresh. With so little space, the stores only stock items that are popular. For poorer people, that means cheap processed foods. The sugar, salt, and fat in those items make them tasty. But they also make the foods fattening and otherwise unhealthy. To find a better selection of healthy foods at a reasonable cost, shoppers might have to travel many miles—a trip that can take several hours if they don't have a car.

Making Choices

By now, your head may be spinning. With so many dangers related to processed foods, what is safe? While the concerns are real, the dangers are not always immediate. According to the U.S. Centers for Disease Control, about 5,000 people in the United States die each year from food-borne illness. By comparison, more than 40,000 die in motor vehicle accidents, and 13,000 die in falls.

It is often difficult to know what you are eating in a restaurant. A restaurant may boast that it makes its own sauce, but it may actually use industrial tomato paste filled with preservatives and HFCS as the base of the sauce.

The real dangers, though, are long term. A constant diet of heavily processed sugars and carbohydrates can lead to obesity and other health risks. Especially at high levels in the diet, substances such as high fructose corn syrup (HFCS) can affect the body's ability to regulate sugar levels in the blood. Food dyes and other additives can have negative effects on children—and on all people, to some degree.

Pizza: Fresh or processed?

There is nothing about pizza that means it has to be unhealthy. Packed with vitamins and antioxidants, tomato sauce is one of the healthiest things you can eat. A whole-wheat crust can provide fiber, and cheese is a valuable source of protein and calcium. Pizza can also be topped with a variety of vegetables, making it a complete meal in one tasty dish.

Unfortunately, pizza can also be turned into a frozen disc filled with unpronounceable ingredients and fat. Frozen pizza is often an example of an unhealthy processed food.

Pizza starts with a crust, and the crust starts with flour. But in a frozen pizza, the wheat in that flour was probably milled, bleached, and enriched long before it made its way anywhere near the pizza.

The frozen pizza is topped with a thick, red tomato sauce. But what exactly is in that sauce, and how does it keep its bright color? There are probably some tomatoes in there, as well as a large dose of HFCS. There is probably also a lot of salt, citric acid, and calcium chloride, acting as a preservative. Odds are good the color comes from a food dye.

Let's assume that the frozen pizza is topped with meat—probably sausage, pepperoni, or some other meat product. As we have seen, how an animal is converted into a uniform meat-like substance is a long, and sometimes horrifying, tale. Moreover, this kind of meat is often full of fat and potentially dangerous chemicals.

The final layer of the frozen pizza is cheese. There is a good chance the cheeses used are "cheese products," which means they probably contain many artificial substances—and are also full of fat.

So, all pizzas are not the same. Think about this the next time you crave one. Perhaps you could have fun making your own, fresh pizza at home. This would allow you to control the ingredients used—and to know exactly what you are eating.

What steps can I take?

While avoiding processed food can be a challenge, there are a few simple steps you can take.

Shop the perimeter

A common suggestion for avoiding heavily processed foods in the supermarket is to "shop the perimeter." The outer ring of a store often contains the least-processed foods, such as fruits and vegetables, meat, dairy, and freshly baked bread. The center aisles tend to contain less-natural creations, such as snacks, cereals, and frozen and instant dinners.

Another option is to shop at farmers' markets. Many farms also sell their produce by the roadside or allow you to pick your own. You can also buy fresh meat and fish from local sources, such as a local butcher or fish store.

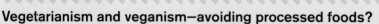

Health watch

Vegetarianism and veganism—avoiding processed foods?

For a variety of health, taste, and **ethical** reasons, many people choose to become vegetarians and not eat any kind of animal flesh. Others, called vegans, choose not to eat any animal products at all, such as dairy or eggs. However, even people who follow these diets have not been able to escape processed food.

Fake meats such as veggie burgers and veggie dogs are popular items for people who avoid meat. However, few people bother to read the ingredients. According to the American Dietetic Association, many "veggie burgers" contain no actual vegetables. Although these products tend to be lower in fat and calories than beef burgers, they may be high in sodium.

The association recommends that people look for "veggie" products with less than 10 grams of protein per serving, as those items tend to contain more vegetables. Higher-protein products are primarily soy and gluten. People with food allergies should read ingredient lists carefully, as many "veggie" products are made from soy, wheat, dairy, and nuts.

Five ingredients

Read the labels. Some nutritionists say you should eat foods that contain no more than five ingredients. While this may be too difficult, the point is clear. If the package lists more chemicals than recognizable ingredients, it is probably processed beyond recognition!

Get involved

The fact that you are reading this book shows that you want to learn more about processed foods and how they affect you. That is a great start. We can change the way corporations treat our food, but only if we make an effort. The first step is to learn more. The next is to act.

Unsing the Internet as a tool, you have access to many resources about food, farming, and product recalls. Many major newspapers have sections devoted to these subjects. Government agencies, such as the FDA in the United States and the Food Standards Agency in the United Kingdom, frequently publish information about food safety, nutrition, and food alerts on their websites.

Vote with your wallet

"Processed" does not necessarily mean bad. Many food manufacturers have responded to consumer concerns by changing how they treat the food they process. There are more and more healthy alternatives in products such as snacks and breakfast cereals. The more consumers buy these products, the more likely manufacturers are to keep making them. At the same time, realize that the word "healthy" on the label does not mean that what is inside the package is necessarily good for you.

Processed foods are a fact of our busy lives. It is nearly impossible to learn everything about every piece of food you put into your body, and as a teenager, you may have little control over what foods your parents do and do not buy. But, as with any issue, the more you know, the better choices you can make. This book is a start. The rest is up to you.

Human Health and Food Chains

The information here may be useful in helping you better understand some of the information contained in the book.

The current USDA food pyramid stresses fruits and vegetables over meat, dairy, and processed foods. Many people object to the food pyramid because it is highly susceptible to political pressure. People representing the beef industry and other food groups pressure those responsible for the pyramid to stress the benefits of the products they represent.

The eatwell plate

Use the eatwell plate to help you get the balance right. It shows how much of what you eat should come from each food group.

Fruit and vegetables

Bread, rice, potatoes, pasta and other starchy foods

Flakes

Meat, fish, eggs, beans and other non-dairy sources of protein

Foods and drinks high in fat and/or sugar

Milk and dairy foods

The "eatwell plate" is the United Kingdom's equivalent of the USDA's food pyramid. It is meant to show how much of different types of food a person should consume.

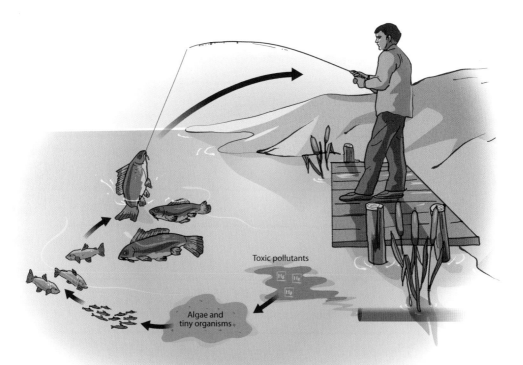

Toxic pollutants

Hg Hg
Hg

Algae and tiny organisms

Because humans eat other animals, they are at the top of the food chain. This in turn means that anything that happens to items lower in the food chain also happens to people. For example, some fish swim in waters that have high levels of mercury, a poisonous metal. The mercury enters their bodies and humans can eat it if the fish are caught for food.

Timeline

Approximately 8000 BCE	beer and bread are the first processed foods
Early 16th century	corn (maize) is grown for the first time in Europe (see earlier note about the date on page 12)
1809	canning process is developed in France to preserve food
1869	artificial butter, called margarine, is invented
1878	Gustavus Swift begins development of first refrigerated rail car to preserve fresh meat
Late 1800s	Robert Koch and Louis Pasteur develop the germ theory of disease
1909	Chicago becomes the first city to ban the sale of unpasteurized milk
1940s	widespread use of vitamin-enriched flour begins in the United States
1950s	chicken nuggets invented
1970s	food companies begin to use HFCS on a wide scale (see earlier note about the date on page 14)
1999	Scientists develop the first strain of golden rice, which contains added vitamin A
2010	Canada declares the chemical BPA a toxic substance, making it easier to limit its use; some New York lawmakers call for a ban on foods containing HFCS

Glossary

additive chemical or other substance added to a food during processing, often used to help preserve the food

antioxidant element that slows or prevents oxidation, a process that transfers electrons from a substance. Oxidation can cause "free radicals," which may cause disease.

bran outer coating of a cereal grain

carbohydrate one of three major nutrients the human body needs to survive, found in fruits, vegetables, beans, and grains

cholesterol waxy substance produced by the body and also found in some foods; high levels in the body can cause heart disease

contamination state of having a harmful or bad substance present

cure treat a food with a chemical or a process that helps preserve it

developed country nation with high average income and large industries

developing country nation in the process of building industries and raising the income level of its citizens

diabetic having the disease diabetes, which results when the body produces too much of, or doesn't properly use, the chemical insulin

E. coli bacteria found in the digestive tract that can cause disease

enrich in food, to add nutrients that were lost during processing

ethics system of beliefs about what are right or wrong actions

fatty acid substance found in some fats that can affect the health of humans

fermentation conversion of sugar to carbon dioxide and alcohol by adding yeast

fiber substance found in grains, fruits, and other foods that aids digestion and has health benefits

fortified strengthened. In food, fortified foods have had vitamins and minerals added to them.

fructose naturally occurring, simple sugar found in honey and many fruits

genetically modified (GM) organism that has had its genes altered to promote certain qualities

germ center part of a grain, found inside the kernel

high fructose corn syrup (HFCS) type of sugar made from corn using an industrial process

homogenization mechanical process that breaks up the cream (fat) globules in milk into very tiny particles, to keep a cream layer from forming

hormone chemical either produced in a living organism or added to it through food or injection, which affects cells

industrialized featuring the widespread use of machines and technology to produce a variety of goods

kernel inner part of a grain used to make flour

labor union group of workers who join together to ensure that they are all treated fairly and equally

mill to take a raw grain and turn it into flour

neurological relating to an organism's system of nerves

nitrosamines harmful chemicals created in the body when nitrites combine with certain proteins

obesity body weight that is much greater than what is healthy or average

organic farming method that does not use chemicals to fertilize crops, also refers to crops produced this way

partially hydrogenated oil oil used in cooking that has been altered so it is solid or partially solid, instead of liquid

pasteurize process of heating milk or other food products to kill bacteria

preservative chemical that helps keep a food from spoiling

protein one of the major chemical nutrients humans need to live

recall removing food products from stores because of a health concern

sanitary clean enough to promote good health

sodium scientific name for salt, which comes in many forms

synthetic made by humans through some sort of chemical process

trans fat type of unhealthy fat found in partially hydrogenated oils

Further Information

Books

Chevat, Richie, and Michael Pollan. *The Omnivore's Dilemma: The Secrets Behind What You Eat.* New York, NY: Dial, 2009.

Ettlinger, Steve. *Twinkie Deconstructed: My Journey to Discover How the Ingredients Found in Processed Foods Are Grown, Mined (Yes, Mined), and Manipulated into What America Eats.* New York, NY: Plume, 2008.

Hawkes, Nigel. *Genetically Modified Foods.* Brookfield, CT: Copper Beech, 2000.

Schlosser, Eric, and Charles Wilson. *Chew on This: Everything You Don't Want to Know About Fast Food.* Boston, MA: Houghton Mifflin, 2007.

DVDs

Fast Food Nation. Beverly Hills, CA: 20th Century Fox, 2007.
This film is based on the nonfiction book by journalist Eric Schlosser.

Food, Inc. Los Angeles, CA: Magnolia, 2009.
Learn about industrial farming in this documentary.

King Corn. New York, NY: Docurama, 2008.
This documentary tells the story of two students who plant an acre of corn and follow it from their farm to the dinner plate—and everywhere else corn appears.

Websites

www.mypyramid.gov

www.eatwell.gov.uk
These U.S. and UK government sites provide interactive resources for better understanding how to choose the best foods to eat.

www.eatlocalchallenge.com
This blog is about how and why to eat local, minimally processed foods.

www.eatwellguide.org
This site helps you find fresh, organic, healthy food near your home.

www.foodsafety.gov
This government site provides lots of food safety information and updates.

Index